# AFGHANISTAN

 **Marshall Cavendish**
Benchmark

New York

Written by: Deborah Fordyce
Editors: Peter Mavrikis, Cheryl Sim
Publisher: Michelle Bisson
Series Designer: Benson Tan

Photo research by Thomas Khoo

Originated and designed by Marshall Cavendish International (Asia) Pte Ltd
Copyright © 2011 Marshall Cavendish International (Asia) Pte Ltd
Published by Marshall Cavendish Benchmark
An imprint of Marshall Cavendish Corporation
All rights reserved.

This publication represents the opinions and views of the author based
on Deborah Fordyce's personal experience, knowledge, and research.
The information in this book serves as a general guide only. The author
and publisher have used their best efforts in preparing this book
and disclaim liability rising directly and indirectly from the use and
application of this book.

Other Marshall Cavendish Offices:
Marshall Cavendish International (Asia) Pte Ltd, 1 New Industrial Road,
Singapore 536196 ● Marshall Cavendish International (Thailand) Co Ltd.
253 Asoke, 12th Flr, Sukhumvit 21 Road, Klongtoey Nua, Wattana,
Bangkok 10110, Thailand ● Marshall Cavendish (Malaysia) Sdn Bhd,
Times Subang, Lot 46, Subang Hi-Tech Industrial Park, Batu Tiga,
40000 Shah Alam, Selangor Darul Ehsan, Malaysia

Marshall Cavendish is a trademark of Times Publishing Limited.
All websites were available and accurate when this book was sent to press.

Library of Congress Cataloging-in-Publication Data
Fordyce, Deborah.
Afghanistan / written by Deborah Fordyce.
p. cm. — (Welcome to my country)
Includes bibliographical references and index.
Summary: "An overview of the history, geography, government, economy,
language, people, and culture of Afghanistan. Includes numerous color
photos, a detailed map, useful facts, and detailed resource section"
—Provided by publisher.
ISBN 978-1-60870-149-0
1. Afghanistan—Juvenile literature. I. Title.
DS351.5.F65 2011
958.1—dc22                    2010000311

Printed in Malaysia
135642

**PHOTO CREDITS**
Agence France Presse: 16, 20, 24, 28, 34, 35, 38, 39
Alamy: 23
Corbis: 3 (center), 27
Getty Images: 4, 21, 25, 32, 36, 37
Getty Images/Hulton Archive: 10 (bottom), 12, 14, 15 (all), 17, 36
HBL Network Photo Agency: 30
Hutchison Library: 1, 2, 3 (top & bottom), 5, 6, 7, 9, 10 (top), 18,
    19 (all), 22, 29, 41 (top), 45
North Wind Picture Archives: 11
Photolibrary: cover, 31
Topham Picturepoint: 8, 13, 26, 33, 40, 41 (bottom)

# Contents

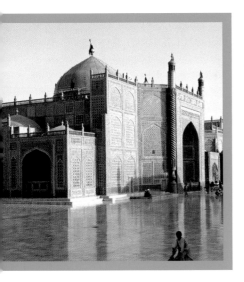

Words that appear in the glossary are printed in **boldface** type the first time they occur in the text.

The giant Buddhas of Bamian were carved into the side of this mountain 1,500 years ago. They were, however, destroyed by the Taliban in 2001.

# Welcome to Afghanistan!

**A**fghanistan is a land of steep, snowy mountains and windy deserts. During its five-thousand-year history, Afghans have often struggled with invaders and with internal conflict. Up until today, Afghanistan is still trying to transform itself into a more stable country. Let's learn more about Afghanistan.

These Afghan children are washing dishes in a stream near their village.

## The Flag of Afghanistan

The flag was adopted in 2004 and has vertical black, red, and green stripes. The white symbol on the middle stripe is a **mosque**, which shows that Afghanistan is a country that follows the Islamic religion.

# The Land

Afghanistan is a landlocked nation surrounded by other countries. Turkmenistan, Tajikistan, and Uzbekistan are located to the north. China lies to the east. Pakistan borders to the east and south, and Iran extends to the west.

High mountains, such as the Hindu Kush mountain range, cover much of Afghanistan. The Hindu Kush divide the country into three main regions: the Northern Plains, the Central Highlands, and the Southwestern Plateau. On the Hindu Kush's northern edge lies the country's highest point, Nowshak Peak.

The deep valleys of the province of Bamian fall between the Hindu Kush and Koh-e-Baba Mountains.

The Konduz River is a major **tributary** of the Amu Darya River.

## Rivers

Afghanistan's major rivers flow from the mountains into the valleys. The Helmand River, the longest river in the country, flows from the Koh-e-Baba Mountains. The Amu Darya River, which starts in a mountain range called the Pamirs, in the northeast, forms a border between Afghanistan, Tajikistan, and Uzbekistan. The lands of the Northern Plains follow the Amu Darya and contain the country's most **fertile** soil.

# Climate

Temperatures in Afghanistan can climb to almost 120° Fahrenheit (49° Celsius) or fall as low as 5° F (−15° C). With ice-cold winds blowing from the north, winters in the northwestern mountains are especially harsh, and snow buries the Northern Plains and the Central Highlands. Summer brings heat and sandstorms to the Southwestern Plateau and **monsoon** rains to the mountain areas in the south. Less than 3 inches (7.5 centimeters) of rain falls each year in the west, while the Hindu Kush range gets about 53 inches (135 centimeters).

Deep snow in the Hindu Kush range and other mountainous areas is the main source of Afghanistan's water supply.

This herdsman watches over his young camels as they graze in the green pastures of central Afghanistan.

## Plants and Animals

War and damage to the environment have hurt Afghanistan's plant and animal life. Many trees, including pine, oak, walnut, juniper, and ash, have been cut down for fuel, reducing forests to only 10 percent of the land.

Wolves, foxes, wild goats, striped hyenas, and snow leopards live in the mountains. About two hundred species of birds live in Afghanistan. Even more stop there during **migrations**.

# History

Humans have lived in Afghanistan for almost 100,000 years. **Archaeologists** believe that the earliest settlers of the Hindu Kush area may have been some of the world's first farmers.

In 135 BCE, five tribes from Central Asia invaded Afghanistan, bringing the Buddhist religion with them. The tribes fought for control, and the Kushan tribe won. Under Kushan rule, the tribes conquered Afghanistan.

This giant statue of Buddha was carved in the fifth century CE. In March 2001, the Taliban government tore it down.

## The Arrival of Islam

In the seventh century CE, Arab armies brought the Islamic religion to Afghanistan, but most people went back to their old beliefs when the Arabs left. The practice of Islam was revived in the eleventh century with the Ghaznavid dynasty's rise to power. Its rulers also spread their faith to Pakistan, Iran, and parts of India.

In 1219, Genghis Khan invaded the country and ruled until his death in 1227. Soon after, Afghanistan broke into smaller states ruled by chiefs or princes. In the late

Alexander the Great brought Greek culture to the many lands he conquered. In 327 BCE, Alexander the Great invaded Afghanistan.

Genghis Khan was one of the most famous conquerors in history. Khan's empire reached from China in the east to the Adriatic Sea in the west. In 1219, Genghis Khan conquered all of Afghanistan.

1300s, new rulers, known as the Timurids, brought a period of peace that lasted a hundred years. After Timurid rule ended in 1507, Afghanistan was ruled mainly by two Islamic powers—the Mughal Empire from India and the Safavid dynasty of Persia (now Iran). By the end of the seventeenth century, a powerful **ethnic** group known as the Pashtuns began to emerge. In 1747, Ahmad Shah Durrani, a Pashtun military commander, formed his own empire which covered present-day Afghanistan, Pakistan, and parts of Iran and India. Today, he is considered by many Afghans to be the founder of their country.

In 1880, politicians from Persia (now Iran) and Britain met in Kabul, which is Afghanistan's capital city.

## More Conflict

War returned to Afghanistan in the nineteenth century as the country was caught between the power struggles of Britain and Russia. Britain went to war with Afghanistan twice and seized control of its foreign affairs. The British were thus able to prevent Russia from having any relations with Afghanistan. They feared that Russia would enter Afghanistan to invade India, which was an important British colony.

By 1901, Britain and Russia had agreed upon Afghanistan's borders, which are still in use today. Even though there was now peace between Britain and Russia, Afghanistan was tired of British influence. In 1919, the third Anglo-Afghan War broke out. This time, the Afghans, under Amanullah Khan, forced the British out of the country and declared Afghanistan an independent nation.

# From a Monarchy to a Republic

Amanullah Khan tried to make the nation more modern, but some of the country's ethnic and religious groups thought his reforms went too far. The disagreement started a civil war in 1928, and Amanullah was eventually overthrown by Habibullah Kalakani in 1929. Kalakani, however, did not stay in power long. Within the same year he was defeated by Mohammed Nadir Shah, who was backed by the British army. Afghanistan then became a **monarchy**, and Nadir Shah became its first king.

The monarchy lasted less than fifty years. In 1973, Mohammad Daud Khan, who was prime minister from 1953–1963, overthrew the monarchy and changed Afghanistan's system of government to a **republic**. He declared himself the country's first president.

In August 1961, Mohammad Daud Khan (**left**), who was then prime minister of Afghanistan, visited Yugoslavia and met with that country's leader, Marshal Tito (**right**).

## Internal Conflict and the Taliban

While Daud Khan tried to **stabilize** Afghanistan, the internal conflict continued, including both nationwide revolts as well as ten years of fighting with the Soviet Union.

In the late 1990s, a group called the Taliban took over in Afghanistan. Under the Taliban's harsh control, the Afghan people, especially women and girls, lost many of their human rights. In 2001, American, British, and Afghan fighters banded together to overthrow the Taliban government.

Afghan soldiers celebrate the return of Zahir Shah, their country's last king. Zahir was forced from power when Mohammad Daud Khan took over. After thirty years in **exile**, Zahir returned to Afghanistan on April 18, 2002.

## Amanullah Khan (1892—1960)

In 1919, Amanullah Khan initiated Afghanistan's third war with Britain. This month-long conflict brought about the country's independence. Because of his unpopular reforms, Amanullah Khan was forced out of Afghanistan in 1929.

Amanullah Khan

## Meena Kishwar Kamal (1957—1987)

A strong supporter of freedom, Meena Kishwar Kamal worked to gain equal rights for women by founding a group, the Revolutionary Association of the Women of Afghanistan. She also worked to end Soviet control in Afghanistan.

## Mohammad Daud Khan (1909—1978)

Mohammad Daud Khan made many educational and social reforms during his ten-year term as Afghanistan's prime minister. After forcing his cousin, Zahir Shah, out of power in 1973, he made Afghanistan a republic. He was killed in a coup led by the Communists.

Mohammad Daud Khan

# The Government and the Economy

After the Taliban government was defeated, members of Afghanistan's main religious, political, and ethnic groups met to discuss the country's political future. They agreed to set up an **interim** government, which included the Afghanistan Interim Administration (AIA). The AIA had thirty members who came from the Pashtun, Tajik, Hazara, and Uzbek communities and several other ethnic groups.

In November 2001, representatives of Afghanistan's major groups met with members of the United Nations (UN) in Bonn, Germany, to create an interim government.

Before becoming Afghanistan's head of state, Hamid Karzai, a Pashtun tribal leader, was head of the AIA. Karzai is currently serving a second five-year term as president after winning the presidential elections in 2009.

## Afghanistan Interim Administration

From December 2001, the AIA was an important part of Afghanistan's interim government. During the time it held power, the AIA changed the country's court system to follow Islamic law. Afghanistan now has an independent **judicial** system headed by the Supreme Court. The AIA directed the interim government until June 2002, when Hamid Karzai was named head of state. In 2004, a new constitution was put in place and Karzai became the first democratically elected president. He was re-elected as head of state in 2009.

The number of fish in Afghanistan's rivers, lakes, and streams is limited, but there are many different kinds. These fishermen are trying to catch fish from a river in the province of Bamian. Villagers usually make their own fishing nets instead of using modern equipment.

## The Economy

Although Afghanistan has abundant natural resources, it is one of the poorest countries in the world. Both the Soviet invasion and the civil war that followed seriously damaged the country's industries and led to short supplies of food and fuel. Since 1999, the country has also lived through a **drought**, which destroyed livestock and reduced crop production, leaving millions of Afghans starving.

# Agriculture and Irrigation

About 70 percent of Afghanistan's workforce is employed in agriculture. Without modern machinery, chemical fertilizers, or pesticides, however, their methods of farming are outdated. Wheat and cotton are the country's main crops. Other crops, including grapes, apricots, figs, and nuts, are commonly sold to other countries. Afghan farmers also raise goats, sheep, donkeys, and camels. The farmers depend on **irrigation** to supply water for crops and animals, but the country's irrigation system has been badly damaged by war and drought.

Poorly developed transportation has added to the economic problems in Afghanistan. In cities, buses and colorfully painted trucks (above) are the main forms of transportation. In rural areas, most people walk or ride horses, donkeys, and even camels.

Tomatoes are one of the kinds of fruit and vegetable crops sold at this market in Kandahar.

# People and Lifestyle

Because so many cultures have come together in Afghanistan, the Afghan people speak many different languages, and follow varied ethnic traditions. The Pashtuns, Tajiks, Hazaras, and Uzbeks are the country's main ethnic groups. The Pashtuns, who live in the south and east of Afghanistan, are the largest ethnic group. They make up almost 40 percent of Afghanistan's population. The Tajiks, the second largest ethnic group, live mostly in the provinces of Badakhshan, Herat, and Kabul.

Because of constant fighting in the cities, many Afghans moved to the countryside. Today, families are returning to the cities, where they can benefit from international aid.

Kochis, or **nomads**, have journeyed between the desert and the mountains of Afghanistan for centuries. Their traveling lifestyle is now more difficult after many years of war and drought.

The Hazaras, the country's third largest group, live mainly in central Afghanistan, while the Uzbeks, the fourth largest group, live north of the Hindu Kush range. Other groups include the Nuristanis, Baluch, Chahar Aimaks, and Kyrgyz. This ethnic mix gives Afghanistan great cultural variety but also creates social and political problems between the groups.

# Family Life

For most Afghans, families are the center of society. Many generations live together, and the oldest male in each household heads the family. Men in the family are in charge of business and agriculture, while the women run the household and raise the children.

It is traditional for Afghan parents to arrange marriages for their sons and daughters. Once a woman marries, she becomes part of her husband's family and leaves her own family behind.

This Pashtun brother and sister, like most Afghan children, are taught about family values, such as respect for their elders, at an early age.

Most Afghan houses have flat roofs. In hot summer weather, many Afghans sleep on their roofs to keep cool.

## Rural and Urban Life

In Afghanistan's **rural** areas, most families live in mud-brick houses. A high wall often surrounds each home or group of homes. Few rural houses have electricity, running water, or even clean drinking water.

Some wealthy **urban** families own houses, but most families live in high-rise apartment buildings. Due to the damage caused by years of war, many urban houses and other buildings have no running water or sewer services.

# Education

In March 2002, many Afghan children attended school for the very first time. More than two decades of war had destroyed schools and forced teachers out of Afghanistan, leaving an entire generation of children uneducated. Today, only 28 percent of Afghans over age fifteen can read and write.

Although the country is rebuilding its school system, the task is not easy. New schools have to be constructed, schoolteachers need to be trained, and teaching materials are in short supply.

This teacher in Herat is helping a boy with his studies. Their classroom is in the basement of a house because, like many Afghan cities, Herat has no school building.

Following the fall of the Taliban, girls are now able to receive an education and women are free to work.

## School Systems

Afghanistan has two school systems: public schools and Islamic schools. Most children attend public schools, where they study subjects such as the Pashto and Dari languages, history, mathematics, and science. They also study the **Koran**.

Islamic schools are run by male religious teachers called **mullahs**, and only boys may attend. Students spend much of their time studying about their faith, but subjects such as reading, writing, and arithmetic are also taught.

# Religion

Afghanistan's official religion is Islam, and its followers are called Muslims. All Muslims are expected to live by the Five Pillars of Islam, a set of religious rules. The first rule is to recite, "There is no God but Allah, and Muhammad is His messenger." The other pillars are to pray five times a day, to donate money to the poor, to fast during each day of the Islamic holy month, and to make at least one **pilgrimage** to the holy city of Mecca, in Saudi Arabia.

This Islamic mosque is located in Kabul. About 99 percent of all Afghans belong to the Islamic religion. Other religions in Afghanistan include Sikhism and Hinduism.

The Blue Mosque, in Mazar-e Sharif, is a famous landmark in Afghanistan. It holds the tomb of Hazrat Ali, the cousin and son-in-law of the prophet Muhammad.

## Mosques

Most Afghan towns and cities have a mosque where Muslims go to worship. Some mosques become holy sites and thousands of Afghan pilgrims travel great distances to visit them. Mosques serve as meeting places, too. After Friday prayers, many people stay at the mosque to visit with friends and relatives. Social and religious festivals also are held in mosques.

# Language

Dari and Pashto are Afghanistan's two official languages. Half of all Afghans, including the Tajiks and the Hazaras, speak the Dari language. The Pashtuns speak Pashto. Educated Afghans often read and speak both languages, but Dari is used most often in business. A small number of Afghans, including Uzbeks, speak Turkic languages.

This street stand in Kabul sells magazines and books. Kabul also has several newspapers. A few of the popular newspapers include *Anis*, written in the Dari language, *Hewaad*, in Pashto, and the *Kabul Times*, written in English.

These Kyrgyz children from northeastern Afghanistan are learning to read the Koran.

## Literature

Poetry has been Afghanistan's most popular form of writing for centuries. Two of the country's best-known poets are Jalaluddin Rumi (1207–1273) and Khushal Khan Khattak (1613–1690). Rumi, who wrote in the Dari language, based his poetry on his Islamic beliefs and on his opinions of Afghan culture. Khattak, who is the country's national poet, wrote about the traditions and laws of the Pashtuns. Today, Afghan authors often write about the years of war in their country and about freedom.

# Arts

Afghanistan's unique artistic style comes from the country's many ethnic groups and mixture of cultures.

## Architecture

Some of the earliest buildings in Afghanistan date back to the time of the Buddhists. Starting in the eleventh century, Islamic architects created majestic mosques, including the Blue Mosque of Mazar-e Sharif. Islamic mosques have dome-shaped roofs and tall towers called minarets. Many people believe Islamic mosques are Afghanistan's greatest works of art.

## Carpets

Afghanistan is also known for its colorful wool carpets, which are made by hand. Carpet colors and designs vary by region and ethnic group. Uzbeki carpets have rows of figures on a red background. Baluch rugs are a mixture of dark colors.

Calligraphy is a valued art form in Afghanistan. It is a kind of elegant handwriting that is often used to decorate the walls of mosques and other buildings. Usually, messages in calligraphy are taken from poetry or from the Koran.

Afghans are known for their pottery. Other important crafts include embroidery and jewelry making.

## Folk Dances

Dancing is an important part of life in Afghanistan. Most Afghan folk dances involve quick hand movements, lots of spinning, and difficult steps. The *attan* (AH-tan) is the Afghan national dance and is performed at religious festivals and weddings. To dance the attan, men stand in a circle, clapping their hands as they move their feet faster and faster.

Afghanistan's women have their own dances. Using facial expressions and hand movements, the dancers tell stories about the daily lives of women.

Afghan folk dances are not only fun to watch but also help preserve the history and traditions of each ethnic group.

This Kyrgyz girl is playing a lute. Two kinds of lutes, the *tanbur* (TAN-bur) and the *dutar* (DEW-tar), are often used to play Afghan folk music.

## Music

Afghan music blends many styles and rhythms and is played with a variety of instruments. The *rubab* (ruh-BAHB) is the country's national instrument. It looks like a banjo and is played by plucking the strings to create short, sharp sounds. Afghan musicians also play many types of drums, which they beat with their palms and fingers.

# Leisure Time

Because of all the hardships in their everyday lives, Afghans do not have a lot of leisure time. Dancing and singing, however, are very popular. Both men and women dance, but they do not dance with each other. Afghan men often get together at teahouses. Besides drinking tea, they exchange news and listen to music.

Afghans also enjoy the ancient art of storytelling. Many Afghan stories and folktales teach traditional values, religious beliefs, or lessons about life.

Chess is a popular game in Afghanistan, especially among men. The chess players are often so competitive that the game lasts all day.

These boys in Kabul are playing street soccer. The game of soccer does not require a lot of equipment, so it is easy for children to play.

## Children's Games

Children in Afghanistan play their own versions of games such as hide-and-seek, blind man's bluff, and tag, which are familiar around the world. They also like to go on picnics and fly kites.

Afghan girls can now play in the outdoors again, which they were prevented from doing during the Taliban's rule. Afghan boys enjoy egg fighting. Each player bumps a hard-boiled egg against an opponent's egg, trying to break the other player's egg. The winner is the last player with an uncracked egg.

## Sports

Playing or watching most sports was **banned** in Afghanistan during Taliban rule. Today, many male and female athletes are training again. Most of the country's sports centers and equipment were damaged or destroyed during years of war, so athletes must practice without them.

## Wrestling

Afghan wrestling is called *pahlwani* (pahl-wah-KNEE). In this style of wrestling, contestants can grab their opponents' arms or clothing, but cannot touch their legs. The goal is to pin an opponent's shoulders to the ground.

Two young Afghan wrestlers compete in a bout at the Ghazi Stadium in Kabul.

Afghan youths play a game of soccer in a stadium in Kabul. Soccer is a popular team sport in Afghanistan.

## Team Sports

*Buzkashi* (BOOZ-kah-SHEE) is the national sport of Afghanistan. Dating back to the 1200s, Buzkashi is a team sport that is played on horseback.

*Topay-danda* (TOE-pay-DAN-dah), a type of stickball, and soccer are two other favorite team sports. Most of the soccer teams in Afghanistan are named for the cities or regions in which the players live. Athletes in Afghanistan are very competitive. Winning is a matter of honor both for the athletes and for their families and communities.

## Religious Festivals

Afghans celebrate many religious festivals. One of the most important is Ramazan, which is also known as Ramadan, the Islamic holy month. During Ramazan, Muslims do not eat or drink in the daytime. They celebrate the end of the holy month with a three-day festival called Eid al-Fitr (EED AHL-fitr). Another important religious festival is called Eid al-Adha (EED AHL-ad-ah), or the Feast of **Sacrifice**. It honors Abraham for offering his only son to God.

During the month of Ramazan, Muslims gather at mosques, such as the Jamae Mosque in the city of Herat, to pray.

A flag is raised in Ziarat-i-Sakhi Ali Square, in Kabul, to celebrate Nawruz. People start preparing for this holiday weeks ahead of time.

## National Holidays

Under Taliban control, most of the national holidays in Afghanistan were banned. Today, Afghans are free to celebrate. The most important national holiday is Nawruz (NOW-rooz), on March 21. It is the Afghan New Year, which marks the beginning of spring. Other national holidays include Labor Day, on May 1, and Independence Day, on August 19, **commemorating** the country's freedom from British control.

# Food

Afghan cooking has been largely influenced by settlers from Pakistan, India, and Iran, who brought many sauces, soups, and spices with them. Afghan meals usually include rice and a flatbread called *naan*. Fruit, cheese, eggs, and chicken are also common foods in Afghanistan. Many dishes are seasoned with mint, dill, and **saffron**.

Grapes are a popular fruit at this market in the city of Herat. Herat is known for its fruits, which grow in the fertile lands that surround the city. Afghans also eat melons, apricots, and pomegranates.

These Pashtuns are eating naan with a yogurt dish. Most Afghans sit on the floor to eat. A cloth or carpet in the center of the floor serves as a table.

The most popular drink in Afghanistan is tea. People living in the north like green tea, while Afghans south of the Hindu Kush usually drink black tea. Both kinds of tea are most often served after a meal or in a teahouse.

Afghans prepare rice in many ways. It is served plain, or with meat, herbs, or sauces. Afghanistan's most popular rice dish is *quabili pallow* (KAH-bih-lee pah-LOW). This dish is prepared by mixing lamb or chicken with onions and rice and topping it with pistachios, almonds, carrots, and raisins. Afghans also eat rice with *korma* (KOR-mah), which is a thick vegetable paste with pieces of meat mixed in.

Other favorite Afghan foods include kabobs—meat and vegetables grilled on sticks, yogurt, noodles, and stuffed pastries filled with potatoes, meat, and spices.

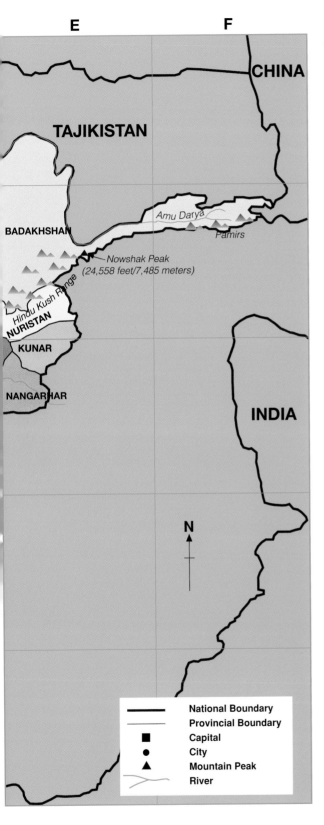

| | E | F |
|---|---|---|

TAJIKISTAN

CHINA

BADAKHSHAN

*Amu Darya*

*Pamirs*

Nowshak Peak
(24,558 feet/7,485 meters)

*Hindu Kush Range*

NURISTAN

KUNAR

NANGARHAR

INDIA

N

National Boundary
Provincial Boundary
■ Capital
● City
▲ Mountain Peak
〰 River

Amu Darya River A1–F2
Badakhshan (province)
   D2–F2
Badghis (province)
   B2–B3
Baghlan (province) D2
Balkh (province) C2
Bamian (province)
   C3–D3
Central Highlands
   (region) A3–D3
China F1–F2

Farah (province) A3–B4
Faryab (province) B2–C2
Ghazni (province)
   C3–D3
Ghowr (province) B3–C3

Helmand (province)
   B3–B5
Helmand River A4–D3
Herat (city) A3
Herat (province) A2–B3
Hindu Kush Range E2

India D5–F4
Iran A2–A5

Jowzjan (province) C2

Kabul (province) D3
Kabul D3
Kandahar (city) C4
Kandahar (province)
   B4–C5
Kapisa (province) D2–D3
Khost (province) D3
Koh-e-Baba
   Mountains C3

Konduz (city) D2
Konduz (province) D2
Konduz River C3–D2
Kunar (province) E2–E3

Laghman (province) D3
Logar (province) D3

Mazar-e Sharif C2

Nangarhar (province)
   D3–E3
Nimruz (province)
   A4–B5
Northern Plains (region)
   B2–E2
Nowshak Peak E2
Nuristan (province)
   D2–E2

Oruzgan (province) C3

Pakistan A5–F2
Paktia (province) D3–D4
Paktika (province) D3
Pamirs F2
Parvan (province)
   D2–D3

Samangan (province)
   C2–D2
Sar-e Pol (province) C2
Southwestern Plateau
   (region) A4–C4

Tajikistan D1–F2
Takhar (province) D2
Turkmenistan A1–C2

Uzbekistan B1–C2

Wardak (province) D3

Zabul (province) C4

# Quick Facts

**Official Name**  Islamic Republic of Afghanistan

**Capital**  Kabul

**Official Languages**  Dari, Pashto

**Population**  28,396,000

**Land Area**  251,827 square miles (652,230 square kilometers)

**Provinces**  Badakhshan, Badghis, Baghlan, Balkh, Bamian, Farah, Faryab, Ghazni, Ghowr, Helmand, Herat, Jowzjan, Kabul, Kandahar, Kapisa, Khost, Konduz, Kunar, Laghman, Logar, Nangarhar, Nimruz, Nuristan, Oruzgan, Paktia, Paktika, Parvan, Samangan, Sar-e Pol, Takhar, Wardak, Zabul

**Major Cities**  Kabul, Herat, Kandahar

**Highest Point**  Nowshak Peak (24,558 feet/7,485 meters)

**Major Rivers**  Amu Darya, Helmand

**Official Religion**  Islam

**National Holidays**  Nawruz (March 21), Labor Day (May 1), and Independence Day (August 19)

**Currency**  Afghani (47.43 AFN = U.S. $1 in 2010)

Snowy mountains and green valleys are both part of the Central Highlands.

# Glossary

**archaeologist:** A scientist who studies ancient peoples and their cultures.

**banned:** Forbidden, usually by law.

**commemorating:** Remembering, often by honoring with a special event.

**drought:** A long period of time with little or no rain.

**ethnic:** Related to a certain race or culture of people who have similar customs and languages.

**exile:** The state of being sent away by force from a person's native land.

**fertile:** Able to support growth or produce offspring.

**interim:** Intended only to last for a short time, until something more permanent is established.

**irrigation:** Supplying water to farm crops using ditches, canals, and pipes.

**judicial:** Related to the enforcement of justice by courts of law.

**Koran:** The holy book of the Islamic religion containing the word of God as revealed to the prophet Muhammad.

**migration:** Movement from one area to another, usually to escape from bad weather or to find food.

**monarchy:** A system of government controlled by a king or queen.

**monsoon:** A strong, seasonal wind that sometimes brings heavy rain.

**mosque:** A building of worship for Muslims.

**mullah:** A Muslim teacher of religion and holy law.

**nomad:** A person who moves from place to place and who often lives in a tent or temporary shelter.

**pilgrimage:** A journey made to a holy place as an act of religious devotion.

**republic:** A country in which citizens elect their own lawmakers.

**rural:** Related to the countryside.

**sacrifice:** Offering something valuable, often an animal or person, to a god.

**saffron:** Part of a crocus flower that is dried and used to flavor or color food.

**stabilize:** To make firm or steady or to make strong enough to survive.

**tributary:** A river or stream that flows into a larger body of water.

**urban:** Related to cities and larger towns.

# For More Information

## Books

Ali, Sharifah Enayat. *Afghanistan*. New York: Benchmark Books, 2006.

Pohl, Kathleen. *Looking at Afghanistan*. Strongville, OH: Gareth Stevens Publishing, 2008.

Weber, Valerie J. *I Come From Afghanistan*. Milwauke, WI: Weekly Reader Early Learning Library, 2006.

Wahab, Shaista and Youngerman, Barry. *A Brief History Of Afghanistan*. New York: Facts on File, 2007.

Whitfield, Susan. *National Geographic Countries of the World: Afghanistan*. Des Moines, IA: National Geographic Children's Books , 2008.

Willis, Terri. *Afghanistan*. Danbury, CT: Children's Press, 2008.

Winter, Jeanette. *Nasreen's Secret School: A True Story from Afghanistan*. New York: Beach Lane Books, 2009.

## DVDs

*16 Days in Afghanistan* (KDK Factory, 2008).

*National Geographic: Lost Treasures of Afghanistan* (National Geographic, 2006).

*The Fixer: Afghanistan Behind the Scenes* (Rockett Media, 2008).

## Websites

**www.afghanistans.com**

Includes informative sections on the country's history, land and resources, fauna and flora, as well as music and even stamps.

**www.embassyofafghanistans.org/kids.html**

Created with kids' interests in mind, this section has information on Afghan children, a slideshow, and a country-themed crossword and word search.

**www.public.asu.edu/~apnilsen/afghanistan4kids/**

A website about Afghanistan created just for children by two Arizona State University professors, who lived in the Afghan capital with their children for two years.

# Index